Promote That Book Now

Julia A. Royston

Edited by: Kaylee Overbey

BK Royston Publishing
P. O. Box 4321
Jeffersonville, IN 47131
502-802-5385
http://www.bkroystonpublishing.com
bkroystonpublishing@gmail.com

© Copyright – 2016

All Rights Reserved. No part of this book may be reproduced, stored in a retrieval system, or transmitted by any means without the written permission of the author.

Cover Design: Vikiana

ISBN-13: 978-0692681541

ISBN-10: 069268154X

Printed in the United States of America

Dedication

I dedicate this book to anyone who has ever dreamed of writing a book, wanted to write a book or is currently writing a book. This book is for you!

Acknowledgement

First, I acknowledge my Lord and Savior Jesus Christ for giving me all of my gifts and especially my gift to write His words.

My husband who is always supportive, loving and encouraging me to utilize all of my gifts and talents. Thank you honey.

To my mother, Dr. Daisy Foree, who is my number one cheerleader and always tells me, "hang in there, you can do it." To my father, Dr. Jack Foree, who is never far away from me in my spirit or heart. I only have to look in the mirror each day to see him.

To Rev. Claude and Mrs. Lillie Royston who support me in everything I do.

To the rest of my family, I love you and thank you for your prayers, support and love.

To my great friend Vanessa Collins who told me to write this book years ago. Thanks for being there with me every step of the way. Love you.

Julia Royston

Table of Contents

Dedication
Acknowledgements
Introduction

What is Promotion?	1
Promoting is Life Changing!	5
Pre-book Launch	7
Diversify Your List	13
Website	15
Support Others	17
Pre-Orders	19
Book Description Teaser	23
Give a Preview	25
Book Trailer	27
Ready Set Launch	29
Promotional Materials	35

Expert/Authority	37
Online Distribution	39
Launch Event	43
Post-Book Launch	53
Email Marketing Sites	55
Social Media	57
Live Events, Conferences, Workshops and Retreats	61
Speaking Engagements	63
Joint Ventures	65
Media	67
Final Word on Promotion	69
Book Promotional Plan	71
About the Author	79

Introduction

Having a great product to sell is wonderful! Having a great product to sell along with correct marketing and promotion is phenomenal and key to launching a successful product, service or project. This book takes the years of helping authors, business owners, educators and ministries with their promotional efforts of their events, products and services. For the past ten years, I have been writing, producing and distributing my own books and music while hosting my own live events. It is not easy and it can get discouraging but how bad do you want it? How much do you believe in what you are selling or promoting? It is much harder to sell something that you don't use, approve or believe in. Sure, professional sales people don't necessarily agree with or even use every product they sell but it is so more effective when you do believe in the product.

I believe in writing, publishing and helping others to achieve their goal of publishing their book. The serious writing bug bit me over ten years ago. I seem to write every single day. I established my publishing business five years ago. After the publishing phase of the book with a client/author, my contract is officially over. Somehow, my clients need and want more from their books, sales and results of publishing their books. Thus, I am venturing more and more into the marketing, promotion and product development of books. How I got here, I really don't know how? But, if given an opportunity, I go for it.

Let's grow together by finding more ways and outlets to not on publish our books but, Promote Our Books Now!

  For the latest updates, conduct your own research and/or reach out to the staff of BK Royston Publishing at www.bkroystonpublishing.com or bkroystonpublishing@gmail.com or call 502-802-5385 for more information.

For information regarding the Write. Publish. Promote Series from Julia Royston, visit: Http://www.writepublishpromoteitnow.com

If while during any part of this process you get stuck or need help, feel free to reach out to us at the mentioned website, email or phone number. We provide individualized publishing, writing and promotional coaching services.

Let the Promoting Begin!

What is Promotion?

Promotion is defined as something devised to publicize or advertise a product, cause, institution, etc. Something such as a brochure, free sample, poster, television or radio commercial, or personal appearance (dictionary.com)

Promotion, to me, is using any means necessary to get the attention of a buyer of your product or service. Whatever it takes to get people's attention and encourages them to buy your product is what should be used.

Once your book is written and published, promotion is the hardest and most important part of the process prior to selling the book.

Throughout this book, I will discuss methods that I have used personally or have seen my authors use as a proven method to promote and launch your book.

Before you even begin the promotion process you need to realize that it is going to take hard work and consistency. You will sell to some people as soon as the book is released and available. This is wonderful, but to have long term sales or to expose your book to new customers then it will take every means possible to promote your book.

Most new authors give up the promotion and sales process right after the initial book signing and that is a mistake. Why? Because there are billions of people on earth who have not heard of your book yet. How will they know about your book if you stop promoting after the initial book signing? There are literally millions of books being published every year. Sure, there will be people who will not be interested in your book and that is fine. But, what about the people who are interested but do not have the opportunity to read your book because you stopped promoting.

We will look at the Pre-Book Launch or Pre-promotion process, the Book Launch process itself, the post book launch and additional promotional tools as well as methods to increase your sales long after the first book signing. Let's begin learning how to Promote Your Book Now!

Julia A. Royston

Promoting is Life Changing!

One question that I ask all authors that I coach or publish is if they are ready? You may think ready for what? And I'm glad that you asked. Are you ready for your life to change after you publish and promote your book? If you are really serious about selling and promoting your book then things in your life will have to change.

First, you will now be a published author. You will have added a new position and title to your name and life. Second, you will now be in the business of writing and finally, you will be a representative and promoter of a product.

You should now be seeking ways and opportunities to promote and sell your book. Promotion and sales and the ability to transact currency all go together. Promoting a product without an outlet to sell it is futile and a waste of your time and effort.

If you are like me and not that good at sales then you will figure it out or otherwise, you won't sell books.

The places where you spend your time may have to change since you will need to spend some time marketing, promoting and selling your book to people with money and an interest in your book.

Promoting takes time and being in the presence of your audience.

Look at your life and see ways, places and people that may have to change in order to properly promote and sell your book.

Pre-book Launch

Congratulations! You have decided to publish a book. You are either self-publishing your book or have been in contact with a publisher.

As soon as you have your exact title, the outline clearly defined and finished then the promotion process begins. It should begin long before the publishing process is complete. You should be establishing yourself as someone who people turn to for information, guidance or encouragement.

You may say that you don't have the book finished yet so why should you even elude to having a book? I'm glad you asked. Curiosity, building momentum and excitement for the soon to be released book is what you want to be creating prior to your book being completed.

Secondly, by telling others that you are writing and will soon publish a book, you have created accountability partners. Once you tell someone, they will be on the lookout and questioning you about when the book will be available. Accountability helps keep you motivated and energized to not let anything stop you from finishing and publishing the book. This also increases the buzz surrounding your book which is what you always want to stimulate and create sales.

Show the Book Cover

As soon as the book's cover is available, begin posting it with a statement that says 'coming soon' rather than an exact date. This can be done as early as three to six months before the actual launch or availability date. If you have had several cover design options, post all three and let your friends, family and followers on social media decide. People love giving their opinions on things such as this. You could even make it a contest. If there are several people that pick the winning cover and the publisher feels that there are too many people to get a free copy then have a drawing for a free signed copy of the book when it is finished.

Build and Engage Your Audience – Stay Connected

Throughout the writing process, when you have the proof copy in your hands and while you may be making changes to your book, make sure that you stay connected with your target audience. Your target audience is the key to making sales of your book. The target audience should have made a connection with you and the topic that you are about to promote. Post encouraging, and engaging, content rich to your social media outlets at least once per day. Even before your book is online and finished, be sure and share the cover image with a quote or other content related teasers daily.

Once your book is finished, ready for sale and posted online, think about if you have promoted it enough for people to buy it. Did you reach out to people enough and speak into their lives enough for them to buy your book? Do you have a following of people that are inspired by you each day? People invest where they feel a connection, receive value, and have a problem solved or a pain that is eased. Have you imparted and invested enough in the lives of others that they would want to invest in you? Business, Books, Ministry, Non-Profits as well as general success in today's society is about building authentic relationships. The exchange of business cards is one thing but after the business card, then what? When there is a mutual benefit and satisfaction in one area then your goal should be for that mutual benefit to transfer into all areas of your business offerings. People should follow you so closely that if you are selling a class, or book, hosting a conference, workshop, or live event then people will want to pay to be a part of it and they should be willing to invite others as well.

If you only have a few people that you engage on social media then it is time to grow your following and find new people. The first 100 books sold could be your immediate family and friends but how are you going to sell more books if you don't make those connections? You can grow your following by paying for ads on social media as well as other promotional resources and outlets that will be listed at the end of the book. You can grow your following by collecting email addresses on your website, blog or social media posts. The amount of money spent on Facebook ads can be minimal but the lasting relationships could be countless.

When you appear in live events, have a notepad or journal with you to collect email addresses. Add those email addresses to your global email list. Connect with people on social media and send them friend requests to make additional connections.

Join private groups and make contributions to the conversation prior to saying that you have a book to sell and people will reach out to you if they feel that you are making a contribution, meeting a need or have solved one of their problems. It's just that simple.

Grow your following so that you will have that many unique people to whom you can promote your book. Do you have a following?

Diversify Your List

If you sold Avon, Amway or Mary Kay many years ago that doesn't mean that you can't take those same clients, customers and contacts to apply to this book signing. I have an email list of people from various parts of my life. I send out emails announcing events to all of my contacts, not just specific people who are interested in books, writing or music. People have multiple interests and their interests change. Since I don't know all of the changes that people have experienced in their daily lives, I send things out to everyone. People who can support do and others share the information to their own contacts.

For example, if people come to a live event and enjoy themselves then they are most likely to come to a retreat. If they come to a retreat that you are hosting then people may come to a party or another celebration that you are hosting. Keep all of your contacts, options, and ideas open to everyone and let them decide what they want to participate in and attend.

Even if you are not hosting the event, but just attending an event gather business cards and make connections with everyone that you come into contact with. You never know who you can partner up with or how you could participate in a joint venture in the future.

Website

You have to have a headquarters for you and your book. Social Media is wonderful but some social media sites will be bought, sold or even vanish. We have seen too often that some social media ideas don't prove profitable and are shut down or go out of business. You don't want that so, you need your own website. Even if the website is just a basic, start-up, do it yourself with a free site such as Wix or Weebly. It is important to have a website so, buy the domain. The domain should preferably be something like your name. If you have a very common name like, John Smith then customize the domain to something like "johnsmiththeauthor.com" or "OhiowriterJohnSmith.com." Whatever works to make your domain name unique, do that and buy the domain. You can use domain.com or godaddy.com or another site that sells domains. You will then use this domain to be applied to your hosting site where your website will be located such as Wordpress, Weebly, or Wix.

For example, the free sites on WordPress can be listed as wordpress.juliaroyston.net. For the customization of your site name and to make it easier for people to find you online, there is a small fee and you can then use your own custom domain at the beginning of the web address. For example, mine is www.juliaroyston.net

Support Others

I admit that it might sound cliché but the old saying, "you scratch my back and I'll scratch yours," is definitely true. If you support other people then it is more likely that they will support you. Just think about it. If people only want you to support them, but they never have the time, effort or money to support you then it is likely that you will not support them. So, if you support someone else, even if it's just by sharing their flyer on social media then you are more likely to gain their support. This is just another way of building a following, and a fan base.

When you support others, you gain ideas, meet new people and see a similar project from a different perspective or vantage point. This is a big reason why I travel. I get to gain information, encouragement and enlightenment from different cultures, people and traditions. I will go to book signings out of town because people do things differently in different parts of the country and world. What better way to expand your knowledge, experience something and impact your community and the world but by seeing something new and supporting others. You will never be the same.

Pre-Orders

Pre-Orders are a way to receive income prior to the book's release, gain interest surrounding your book and gauge how many books will be sold. Pre-orders are also a way to promote your book. The instant that you reveal your book cover to the world, social media or to a close friend, you have begun your promotional efforts. Pre-orders bring in income but pre-orders can also be a part of the promotional process.

Pre-sales or pre-orders work best when you are sure that the book is finished and have a guaranteed time that the book will be finished. You want to make sure that you can actually deliver by this specified date. You want these customers to stick around for your future projects. Unforeseen things can happen with weather and delivery but if you know in advance that you haven't submitted your book to the publishing company or printer in August then don't advertise for pre-orders to be delivered in

September. Advertise that pre-orders are being taken but, delivery should be in October. By this time you will have approved the proof copy and have time to make any corrections or changes prior to going to print. I always produce a proof for my books and my client's books. It is imperative. The printing process is so tricky and the online digital proofs don't do justice to what the final book will look like in your hands.

I don't advocate using pre-orders to finish paying for your publishing costs. If you use the pre-order sales to pay for publishing then how will you buy books? Pre-orders should pay for what it they are intended, the book order.

I have not seen pre-orders work successfully with a first time author because since you have never written a book before people will have no confidence that you will publish or even finish your first book.

Now, after you have been successfully publishing books on a topic of interest with a cover that is attractive and have a track record of delivering books on time, pre-orders are a good way to go for you.

For best results, have the image of a very colorful and attractive book cover on a very appealing and professionally created flyer or postcard on your website for quick and easy payment. Make sure that there is a follow up email to let the customer know when to expect the book, if it will be autographed as well as if there is a problem with the book, and how to contact your customer service department.

You may want to include a special offer on your final book signing event or other occasion as a sign of appreciation for their confidence in you by pre-ordering the book. If possible, include a little token, sticker, bookmark or something extra inside the book package to say thank you. Pre-orders are a leap of faith on behalf of the customer. There is no physical book yet and they are trusting that you will produce what you say you will even if they can only see an image of the book cover.

Book Description Teaser

You have shown the book's cover on social media and it most likely created a lot of buzz and commentary. Some people will say that they love the book's cover, but inevitably someone will ask, what's the book about? The cover may not reveal exactly what the interior of the book is about. For this, you need an informative but enticing book description. If the book is fiction, don't give away the whole plot but describe the details just enough for someone to want to open the book and then buy it.

You will need this book description for the back of the paperback or hardbound book, the online distribution listings, printed on any promotional materials and on your website, blog or social media outlets.

Once you have a good book description, condense it further into three or four word phrases. For example, my romance fiction book, Jillian can be described as follows,

"Jillian is a single, professional woman's love story." The details of where she lives, what she looks like and what she does for a living can be found in the story but that sentence gives a very brief synopsis of the book.

Give a Preview

Word of mouth is still one of the most powerful promotional tools ever. People who read the book and tell others about how much they liked it will generate more customers quicker than any other promotional tool. People want to purchase a book that has been recommended as a winner.

Offer preview copies of your book in exchange for a review or comment about how they liked your book. Ask permission to post the review or comment and watch the engagement by new and repeat readers. Another way to do this would be for them to post their comment or review on their own social media outlets. Offer support to these reviewers in some way by promoting one of their products or services.

Word of mouth promotion works to build a wider audience and attract customers that you may or may not be able to reach on your own.

Book Trailer

There is nothing like seeing a preview or trailer of a new movie or television show. The objective is to make sure that people are enticed, interested and captivated by the book's contents enough to buy it or pre-order it. There is so much research on the power of video that a video book trailer should be considered to engage more readers to your book.

There are several options for video creation software. If you see a book trailer that you like on social media, reach out to the author and find out who produced it and what software they used. Most people enjoy visuals. Be sure to utilize all types of promotional tools and resources to get the word out about your book, but video, audio or any image is key to sales and exposure to your book.

Ready Set Launch

When the book is finished, the proof copy is approved and you are waiting on your order of books, keep promoting just like you would if you had the final books in your hand.

Keep the book fresh in the face and mind of your potential customer.

Invite and remind people about an upcoming book event where they can buy the book, meet you and talk about the book process.

Preview portions or quotes from the book.

Make sure that all is order with your links, headquarters website and your online payment software. You may have to try out the links yourself or have a friend try them out to make sure that they work. You have a small, short window to capture the attention of your customers so that they can buy your book.

The Best Promoter is You!

You are the best promotional outlet for your book. People want to meet the author and feel a connection prior to buying the book. You can have other people help promote you and be at your events along with you to sell for you, but people still want to meet the author.

I recently had an event where I was a vendor. I had paid the vendor fee and I fully trusted the people at my table. I had a scheduling conflict and I was unable to be at the table but a few hours. There was nothing wrong with the person at the table or their capabilities, but people wanted to meet me. When people didn't see me at the table, they didn't come by. When I was at the table in the evenings, the people came and made more purchases. How do I know this? When people saw me at the event in the evenings, they mentioned that they had stopped by earlier to see me. I explained the situation and they understood, but those thirty second conversations made the difference between them being handed a business card and me receiving their credit card for a purchase.

When you promote your own book or books that makes you an inspiration to others, authenticates you as an expert on your topic and if done correctly, motivates people to go to their wallet and make a purchase.

Celebrities that appear in movies go on promotional tours all of the time. They speak about how it was working with the other actors, inspiration for the characters, how they liked the location, director and even their salary.

The celebrities are the best promoters of their upcoming movie. The movie trailer is nice, reviewers are great and critiques may help but there is something about the actual actors in the movie doing the promotion that helps push the movie so that people actually go see it.

After the many decades of movie making, they still have promotional tours in spite of technology. Books and other creative projects are no different. Promotion that is done by the actual participants, creators and producers of a project or event is still the most effective.

Some tips for promoting your book:

1. **Keep a book with you at all times.**
2. **Always have a device that will allow people to purchase your book.**
3. **Keep a business card, brochure or post cards on hand that advertise your book. Some people may not buy the book today but will want information on how to buy the book tomorrow.**
4. **Practice in the mirror or with a family member on what to say if asked about your book. You have probably met wonderful sales people throughout your lifetime. Ask them for tips on how to make best sales pitches.**

5. **Create a one minute speech about your book giving the condensed summary and highlights of what the book is about.**
6. **Be able to relay specifically how someone can purchase the book online. Amazon.com, Barnes&Noble.com, your website or online distribution outlet.**
7. **Finally, you have to tell someone that you have a book and not keep it to yourself. People can't buy what they don't know about.**

Promotional Materials

Whether this is your first book or one hundredth book, you need promotional materials for your book. Put the book cover on a post card with a description on the back and where to purchase the book online. Put the book cover on a business card and put the purchase information on the back of the business card. Traditionally, authors have designed book marks, flyers, posters or one sheets with the information on the card but have something for the reader or customer to have in their hands if they do not purchase the book on site and want to purchase it at a later date. Also, the promotional materials can be given to corporations, non-profits, churches or other outlets to promote your book for you. That's what promotional materials are for, to help you promote your book, its contents and hopefully, sales. These promotional materials don't have to be in the thousands of dollars and you don't have to print thousands of them but have some on hand especially in the pre-sales of your book or at the very beginning of your book launch.

Use an online source like VistaPrint or go to your local staples, OfficeMax, or office depot to have some promotional materials printed within your budget and to your liking.

These promotional materials can be included in a physical media kit or included in an electronic media kit. Make sure that your website, email, phone number, links to the distribution outlets, all social media and any other links to purchase the book are listed on all of the promotional materials.

This eliminates people from saying that they would have bought the book but didn't know where or how to buy it.

Expert/Authority

If your book has a topic surrounding a social or community issue then you should be active and have a voice in your community surrounding this particular issue. Having a book on a particular topic now makes you an expert, authority or advocate about that particular subject, topic or issue. Another way besides the book to add credibility to you as an expert, is to be outspoken and recognized as a leader in your community on your particular topic.

As a publisher, I attend book signings of other authors, I host workshops, conferences, retreats and online events regarding writing, publishing and promoting the business of the publishing industry. In addition to my support, I am an author of more than twenty-five books. I am committed to the industry and have a vested interest in its success. My credibility as a publisher and writer wouldn't carry much weight without it. It is hard to encourage others to write, publish or promote, if I never do it myself. It is hard to tell others to attend live events, pay vendor fees or host workshops, if I never do it. People believe what you do far more than what you say.

Online Distribution

Createspace - Amazon

Online distribution is key to a book launch and future sales of your book. If you do not have online distribution, I will suggest that you hold off on your book signing until you do. There will be people who are unable to attend your book signing because their schedule won't permit or they don't live in your area. Social media allows for global promotion and not just local. You are, in essence, promoting and selling your book, globally and you are not limited to your local event.

In my book and videos titled, Publish Your Book Now, I showed you how to upload your manuscript to Createspace.com. Createspace is owned and operated by Amazon to help people self-publish and distribute their own books. There are many self-publishing sites, but Createspace is the one that I have used most frequently.

Createspace offers expanded distribution to bookstores and other online distribution outlets through Amazon's many distribution outlets. I encourage you to provide a link to your book on Amazon for people to purchase around the globe. The book will be printed and delivered directly to the buyer's door.

Barnes&Noble.com has a distribution arrangement with Amazon through Createspace. When you upload your manuscript to Createspace and select expanded distribution, your book will be available for sale on Barnes and

Noble's website as well. When your book is available for sale on Barnes&Noble.com then you should provide a link to purchase your book there as well.

Kindle and NOOK

We live in the digital world. We can obtain so much information via our phones, computer and other mobile devices. You will miss out on sales and a vast purchasing audience if you do not have your book available in digital format.

If possible, have your book converted to eBook before your book even launches to gain the largest and most varied audience. For example, if you went to the grocery store and wanted to buy potatoes, the large grocery chains have potatoes in a varied format. You can buy frozen potatoes, raw potatoes or potato flakes. The grocery store doesn't miss out on a sale because they didn't have the potatoes in the format that the customer desired. In fact, with just this example, I have given you three streams of income for just potatoes. Imagine all of the other products that the grocery store offers, it is endless.

Therefore, I suggest that if your budget doesn't permit converting your book prior to the book launching then you convert your book as soon after the book launch as possible. You are missing out on a stream of income and customers by not having your book available for purchase in the additional formats. Again, don't miss out on multiple streams of income. If you do not know how to convert your book to eBook format, BK Royston Publishing offers that service. To have your book converted to eBook format, contact us at www.bkroystonpublishing.com or bkroystonpublishing@gmail.com or call us at (502)-802-5385.

Launch Event

Book Signings or other Book Release Events

Because I publish other author's books, I am often asked for advice on book releases, book launch celebrations or book signings as they are traditionally called. In the past, I have said that it is left up to the author, their budget and their desires. Over time, since I have been asked so much, I thought that I would offer some suggestions.

Book first then Celebration - Don't set a book signing date until the book is finished, proof copy of the book is approved and you have a tentative date of when your book order will arrive. Don't set a date until you have the books. I have had an author set a date for the celebration when the book wasn't finished. In this case, it worked out and the books arrived a full week prior to the event but I still don't advise it. The books had to be ordered with expedited delivery which was more of an expense.

Budget – First, budget for the books. There is no need to spend hundreds of dollars on a book release event when you can only afford to pay for ten books to sell. Figure out a budget for the books. I suggest a minimum of one hundred books to start. You should be able to make a list of at least fifty people who will buy your first copies of your book. A few of my authors have started with as many as two hundred to five hundred copies because they had a marketing plan, large fan base, or an exciting topic that was in high demand. They travelled consistently and their books would be able to be sold in multiple markets.

Second, consider your budget for the celebration. The venue, if you will serve food and marketing and promotion of the event must be considered in the celebration budget. Do not charge for the event unless it is a celebration that is going to include food, a workshop, or conference. The purpose of the book celebration is to sell the book. Do not charge to get into the event and charge for the book as well. Charge for admission to the event but include the book as a part of the admission fee. I have seen people charge for admission to cover the cost of the food but then be left with unsold books because people made a choice to eat rather than buy the book. The book should have been included in the cost of admission.

When you are considering the budget for the celebration, cut back on food and have cake and punch in order to emphasize the purchase of the book. Utilize a free or very inexpensive venue and focus on the book. If you release your book in the summer, host a cookout or barbecue at your house or in the park because these venues are free. Sell the book and give away a hot dog. Be creative and use your imagination.

Another idea is to host your celebration at an event that is related to the theme surrounding your book. For example, if your book is a book of poetry, appear at a spoken word event, ask the host if you can mention your book and have a table to sell your book. To benefit the spoken word event, offer to market and promote that event on your social media sites, website or other media outlets. Collaborate and celebrate!

Another idea is to not have an expensive or expense filled event at all but to announce the availability of your book wherever you are. In essence you are having multiple release parties and book signings all over the country. Everywhere I speak, sing or attend an event, I have a book signing because my books, music, publishing and coaching information and products are with me all of the time.

There are several options it all just depends on what you want to do. The last two book signings that I have attended were held in a church in connection with their conference based on the book. I have held a book signing myself at a restaurant that had private rooms. The restaurant's requirement was that I order $100 worth of food in exchange for the use of the room for two hours. I paid $100 for the appetizers, I needed minimal decorations because the restaurant already had decor. People came, bought my book, ate appetizers and left. I walked away after two hours and there was no cleanup for me or my team. It doesn't have to be complicated, just convenient with good parking, relatively good food and your book. Be sure and bring change and make sure that you a way for people to pay with credit card.

Book signing/Book Launch Necessities

Multiple Payment Methods – Offer multiple ways to accept payment. Cash only may be great for you but not everyone carries cash everywhere they go. Be able to accept cash, checks and credit cards.

Carry Change – Make sure that you go to the bank before a book signing and get change even if it is $50 in five dollar bills. Be able to make change.

Don't spend all of your profits – Over the years, I have learned that I must pay debt, re-invest, save and store some of the profits from all of my businesses. First, I must be able to pay any expenses that I incurred for the event. I consider these expenses from the beginning of the planning stages. I either save the money that it will cost or prepare for the expenses of the event. Do not plan on sales of the event to pay for the expenses. Prepare for the expense up front. It is best to not owe debt for event planners, venues, decorations, etc. because you may need these people to help you in the future. Don't disappoint people that you asked to help you plan the event because these are people that can help advertise your future events, your book and promote you as a reputable person. Don't promise what you can't deliver. It will hurt you in the future.

Second, you will need to hold some money to re-invest in more books. I have had an author sell out of books at the event but spent the money made on the sell and it was a long time before money was available to buy more books. The customers were disappointed because they wanted to purchase the books from the author and have them autographed rather than buy them online. The momentum and interest surrounding the book was lost and it would take months to rebuild. Hold some profits from the book sale to purchase more books.

Third, hold some of the small cash bills for change for the next event. I deposit the larger bills for book purchases and have a special pouch for change for future events. There are times that I have several events back to back so this comes in handy when in towns that don't have my bank branch or when it's the weekend and the bank is not open.

Fourth, save some money. I have had to learn this method over the years. Save some of the profits just because. Profit should just be that, profit. I should have something to show for my labor, celebration or book business. Being an author is a business. All of your profits shouldn't be lost and spent but some should be saved. You should have sales goals and profit goals. What are yours?

Something commemorative from the event – In addition to the book, each person should get a bag, pen, button or memento from the event. Put some chocolate kisses in a pouch with your business card attached. If the event is in the winter, get some hot chocolate packets and staple your business card or wrap it in the flyer of your upcoming event, teleseminar or workshop surrounding your book. Keep the momentum going even after this book signing.

Have a sign-up list for everyone who attends whether they buy a book or not. If there is someone who mentions that they want to write a book, forward that information to your publisher.

Introduce your publisher or their representative to other people at your event. You never know if secretly people want to write a book but don't know where to start. You have completed the process and someone else may be ready to start the publishing journey.

Have others who have helped and supported you speak on behalf of you and your work speak. If you have people read your book prior to release, have them speak about how well they liked your book.

Post-Book Launch

After the book signing, thank everyone via a personal email, posts on social media, post a message on your website, post the pictures and if a video is created of the event, post that as well. Don't forget to post all of your sales outlets, website links, social media contacts, email and phone number on the thank you posts just in case someone didn't come to the event but still wants to purchase a book.

Just because the initial book signing event is over that doesn't mean that you stop promoting your book. Continue to promote your book periodically on all of your social media accounts and your website but look for more ways to connect your book and outlets for people to purchase your book.

Website

If you did not get a website created prior to the book launch, create one now. Social media is a great way to promote your book while it is being launched but you need a headquarters for you and all of your future books. Create a website for your customers and clients to stay up to date with all of your upcoming events and to purchase your book directly from you rather than from a distribution outlet which increases your profits. Don't eliminate any of your online distribution outlets but this will be an additional distribution outlet for the sale and promotion of your book.

As mentioned above, there are many websites that help you create a website, free, quickly and easily

Email Marketing Sites

To keep in contact with your new customers for future events, services or to purchase more copies of your book, subscribe to an email marketing service such as GetResponse or Constant Contact. These email marketing services allow you to keep and organize your email contacts. You can create and customize emails, newsletters and flyers to advertise directly to your customers. After the book is launched and the book signing is over, you still want to keep in contact with these customers with encouragement, inspiration and advertisement of any new products, services or events that you will be appearing in for their continued support.

Julia A. Royston

Social Media

We have mentioned social media several times throughout the book but be sure to always be looking out for new ways to address your current audience and get in front of a new audience. Video is an effective way to promote to audiences. Whether you use Periscope, Facebook Live or YouTube, have a video presence. Practice using your phone and create short videos. If you are targeting a younger audience, use snapchat for short quick videos about your book or service.

Remember, you are keeping in contact with people who have already purchased your book but you also need new customers to purchase your book in order to increase your sales.

Social Media Groups

There are all types of social media groups that assemble to talk about similar problems, gain solutions and share ideas. Search for and join a social media groups that are interested in the topic surrounding your book. Be sure to review the group's rules for posting, sharing links and advertisement. You can easily be removed from a group if you don't follow the rules. Do a search for groups on Facebook and LinkedIn, especially. I have gained clients, mentors and new important information from being a part of social media groups.

Audience Hang Outs?

You should dominate where your primary audience hangs out. So, determine who your target audience is and where they hang out or spend time online. Be strategic about your target audience and don't waste money on ads unless you are sure that your target audience logs into that social media site. Don't sleep on any gender or demographic when promoting on these sites but log onto the website that you feel most comfortable with.

I have a presence on all of these sites but feel most comfortable on Facebook and Periscope. I enjoy both of these formats the most but have a social media management software that allows me to post on multiple sites at once. The one I use the most is Hootsuite but another one to try is IFTTT.com.

Live Events, Conferences, Workshops and Retreats

Like politicians, you have to go and take your books to where the public is hanging out and gathering. It is amazing during election time how politicians show up where people are gathered especially when it is a large number of people. As a published author, you have to do the same thing. Make appearancess at live events, conferences or workshops. If your budget allows, pay for a vendor table, sponsorships or ad in a program booklet. You are in business and advertisement is a part of doing business. People can't buy what they don't know about. You have to get out there and "shake hands, kiss babies and sell books" it's just that simple. Books don't sell on their own.

Speaking Engagements

Books sell the most when you speak. That's my mantra about promoting and selling books and I am sticking to it. Sure, your first event will bring sales but that is only the beginning. How do you continue to gain more sales? One way is to speak at events, conferences, workshops and rallies. Make sure that you are a pleasant, information rich and engaging speaker. Don't bore people and cause them to be turned off from your book. That's not the purpose of speaking to sell books. The purpose of speaking to sell books is that the excitement that you create on stage will cause people to leave their seats, find your vendor table and then buy your book. Be sure to promote your book sometime during your speech. Whether you say that you have a book before you speak, refer to the book during the speech or let people know that you have a book after your talk, just be sure and let them know that you have a book, and where you are located. Encourage them to stop by to say hi.

A freebie or give-away

At fairs, carnivals or street events, have you ever signed up to win something free? The free item may not even be related to what the company actually sells but they now have your contact information to reach out to you to via email, phone call or snail mail. This way they can give you additional information about their products or services. The hope is that someone will be a potential buyer. This is not a cold call but a warm call because they have been in contact with you.

"Sign-up here to win a $10 gift card to ___" fill in the blank. See if you don't get people to sign up. It works. Try it and promote your book while the person is filling out the form.

Joint Ventures

Relationships are critical to any endeavor, especially selling books. You can always get more accomplished with the help of a group, team or partnership. In my experience, you have to be strategic, careful and cautious about whom you partner or have a joint venture with. Why? Because the people you associate with are a reflection of you, your character and your behavior, if you do not combine forces with an organization or an individual that is committed to providing similar services then you could end up exhausted and burned out.

First, find joint ventures that are mutually beneficial. Second, have a written agreement regarding the terms of your partnership. Verbal agreements can be vague, causing friction and confusion, especially if one party seems to benefit more than the other party. Be sure to make the terms of the agreement clear and definitive. If you agree to a one year partnership, stick with that. If you agree to a long term joint venture, be sure to have a "get out" clause or a way to be released from the agreement. Require a thirty day written notice to be relinquished from a joint venture.

In addition to the terms of your agreement, sit down and determine the duties, responsibilities, risks, how profits will be dispersed and the role of each member of the joint venture.

Finally, do not enter into a joint venture for the sake of saying that you are in a joint venture. Make sure that the people you choose to joint venture with have the same goals, speak to the same audiences, and offer complementary products and services so that the end result of the joint venture will be profitable and beneficial for all involved parties.

Media

Media attention whether traditional radio, internet radio or tradition television allows an author a wider reach to an audience. Given that most traditional television stations pre-record all of their programs, you will not only reach their live viewing audience, but their online audiences as well. Imagine the potential sales if you advertise in front of these audiences. Simple, right? Not really, but very possible. You have to be ready for media on any level, but with your book listed on your website and online distribution sites in place, reach out and pitch your book to the media.

You will need a media kit and/or one sheet to present to the media. The media kit should include your contact information, information about your book, photos and other pertinent information to make you a desirable guest. The one sheet is a condensed version of your media kit on one sheet of paper. The attention span of media personnel must be quick, concise, neat and eye catching. You don't have more than two minutes to grab their attention. If they desire more information then they will reach out to you. Make sure that your contact information is correct. You never know what television, radio or online outlet will contact you.

Television personalities provide contact information directly on the screen as they report the news or during the course of their programming; whereas, radio personalities provide their contact information on their perspective websites or give it to their listeners while on the air. Reach out to these media personalities. You won't know until you go for it.

Final Word on Promotion

As much as we would love for the book to literally sell itself, this doesn't happen. You have to be the engine, motivation or driving force behind the success of your own book. If people don't know about it then they can't buy it. It would be a shame to have written a bestselling book but have a poor promotion plan for getting that book to the world.

Schedule time each day to promote. If you don't spend the time to promote, then people won't spend the time to buy.

Below is a promotional planning outline. Use it consistently and wisely. Let's Promote!

Book Promotional Plan

If you adhere to the terms that we have talked about in this book, you are well on your way to creating and completing a promotional plan for your book.

Use the following checklist/strategic guide as your plan of action. How you use the template for the book promotional plan is left up to you. If you want to use the template provided and create your own way to write it down then that is still left up to you. The old saying is that if you don't have a plan to succeed then you are planning to fail. Here is simple template of a promotional plan for your book with space to add due dates to help keep you on schedule. You should make sure that each task is completed prior to promoting and releasing your book. Good Luck!

Julia A. Royston

Book Marketing/Promotional Planning Tool

Who is your audience? Who did you write the book for?

Where does your audience hang out the most on social media? Determine which place they hang out in the largest numbers.

What is your budget for promotion of your book? Your budget will determine when, where and how you promote your book. Without a budget or limit to your funds, you can spend thousands of dollars and not produce any results. Get a budget and stick to it. You budget doesn't have to be large but the larger the budget the more places you can promote. Remember that you can promote on social media with a limited budget with the help of your friends, family and followers.

Do you have a blog, newsletter or consistent topics that you post on the Internet? What topics do you write about that would be of interest to the book's audience? What other blogs, Internet radio or television outlets promote these same type of topics or books on their shows? List these internet or traditional outlet media and request to be a part of their shows. Note: make sure that you have a media kit that contains sample questions, topics of expertise and other writing including books and articles as well as a picture gallery from a professional photographer and not a selfie in the bathroom mirror.

Make a list of everyone that you know. Reach out to everyone on this list as a possible customer for your book. If you don't have their full contact information, be sure to get it. The current book that you are promoting may not be the first or the last and you may need to contact them again.

Reviews or Evaluations from readers. Obtain proof copies of your book and recruit people to read and review your book. Only give a proof copy to someone that will follow through and actually review your book. The objective is to get a review or quote about how they liked your book as well as permission to publish their response. Have a way for the person to easily return the review, quote or evaluation of your book. Use a Google form or have them email it directly back to you. People look at reviews to help them decide whether to buy a book or not. Reviews are 'word of mouth.' Where can you get reviews? Who will review your book? Make a list of possible reviewers.

Besides a current list of people that you know, how will you get email addresses or contact information from people that you don't know? Email marketing is key to building, responding to and keeping your own list of contacts without social media.

https://www.standoutbooks.com/13-steps-to-write-a-book-marketing-plan/

Promotional Resources

Amazon Author Page

Good Reads

Literary Hub

Book Talk

Bookbuzzr

PR Log

Free Press Release

Productivity Tools

www.vistaprint.com

www.canva.com

www.zoom.us

www.paypal.com

www.squareup.com

www.Google.com

www.weebly.com

www.wordpress.com

www.wix.com

www.godaddy.com

Articles and Online Groups

http://dianaurban.com/productivity-tools-all-writers-should-know-about

https://www.standoutbooks.com/13-steps-to-write-a-book-marketing-plan/

Join *See ya on the Net* Promotion Group on Facebook

Write. Publish. Promote That Book Now Series.

About the Author

Julia Royston is an author, publisher, speaker, teacher and songwriter residing in Southern Indiana with her husband, Brian K. Royston. To her credit, Julia has written original music for five CDs, two DVDs, authored twenty-eight Books, and served as a contributing author for three books. Julia and her husband spend their spare time overseeing the operations of three companies and a non-profit organization. BK Royston Publishing, LLC and Royal Media Publishing to provide quality, informative, inspirational and entertaining materials in the global market place in all media formats. Julia Royston Enterprises is a writing and business consulting firm to assist aspiring authors and business owners get their message to the masses. For the Kingdom Ministries is a non-profit organization that is established to encourage, enlighten and empower people to live the abundant life and walk in purpose and destiny. By profession, Julia is a certified, technology teacher with the local public school system. For more information visit www.bkroystonpublishing.com, www.royalmediaandpublishing.com, www.juliaroystonenterprises.com or www.juliaroyston.net.

Keep up with Julia on Social Media by following or liking her pages on Facebook, Twitter, LinkedIn, Instagram, Youtube Channel and Periscope.

www.ingramcontent.com/pod-product-compliance
Lightning Source LLC
Chambersburg PA
CBHW071201090426
42736CB00012B/2413